The overwhelming argument for a P&C Insurance Agency to have a current business plan:

A business is a promise to consumers that your company will deliver certain products and services in a professional, knowledgeable, and efficient manner.

A business without a business plan is a business that is making promises that it has spent very little time preparing to keep.

The same holds true for a business that has employees. The employees are depending on and clinging to the promise that the business will provide a stable work environment and a steady paycheck if the employee does what the leaders in the business asks them to do. Again, a business without a business plan is not prepared to deliver on those promises.

Inspire a Nation Business Mentoring Svc.
www.inspireanation.org

Insurance Agency Business Plan Questionaire

Copyright 2013, 2016 Billy R. Williams, PhD and Inspire a Nation Business Mentoring
www.inspireanation.org

This version of the Insurance Agency Business Plan Questionaire was created specifically for a Property and Casualty Insurance Agency by Billy R. Williams, PhD., of Inspire a Nation Business Mentoring Svc. (www.inspireanation.org) and is best when used in conjunction with the Inspire a Nation Business Mentoring Membership Program.

Our membership program has implementation strategies, job-aids, step-by-step processes, scripts, forms, and documents, that address weaknesses identified in this business plan template.
www.inspireanation.org

Disclaimer

We are a mentoring company, not a legal firm. We can discuss generalities and recommendations for using Inspire a Nation Business Mentoring Processes in ways that are consistent with our understanding of the laws. Our training is not a substitute for you obtaining competent, specific legal advice on any of the subjects covered in the training, scripting, and implementation of process suggestions.

In some cases there may be, federal, state, or local laws as well as specific carrier guidelines that may alter, impact, enhance, or supersede the way Inspire a Nation teaches and recommends a process. Our training does not address these issues – again, specific legal advice should be sought to ensure compliance.

While Billy R. Williams PhD and Inspire a Nation Business Mentoring Svc. have used their best efforts in preparing this business plan template, they make no representation or warranties with respect to the accuracy or completeness of the contents of this business plan and specifically disclaim any implied warranties of merchantability or fitness for a particular purpose, and shall not be liable for any loss of profit or any other commercial damages, including but not limited to special, incidental, consequential, or other damages. The advice and strategies herein may not be suitable for your situation.

Table of Contents

Why Businesses Fail?

According to a joint study completed in July of 2013 by Bradley University and the University of Tennessee, 60% of all start up businesses fail within the first 36 months.

Insurance is an industry that does better than most, only 40% of insurances agencies close up shop within the first 36 months.

The study also lists the top reasons for business failure, and they are:
1. Lack of a clear business focus
2. Lack of a business plan
3. Lack of managerial experience
4. Lack of experience in the chosen field of business
5. The business is underfunded
6. Non payment of taxes
7. No experience in record keeping
8. Lack of financial responsibility to creditors
9. Unsuccessful marketing and advertising
10. Underestimation of time and resource requirements

Ladies and gentleman, a good business plan will force you to spot the strengths and shortfalls of your business. This will help keep you from being blind-sided by items that you as the business leader should have been aware of.

Notes about the Business Plan Questionnaire

In an effort to produce what we feel will become the industry standard for the creation of a P&C insurance agency business plan, (in addition to creating the most thorough and accurate plan for your agency) we ask 100's of questions divided into the sections of the plan. It is extremely important that you are honest and accurate when answering the questions!

The business plan consists of narratives that explain important details about each section in the plan and questions that force the agency to thoroughly look at and assess all of its operations. It is my intent to make the creation of an agency business plan as easy as possible. I accomplished this by using *Yes* and *No* questions to make up the bulk of the assessment process.

The questions are asked in a way that allows YES answers to be viewed as agency strengths and NO answers to be viewed as agency weaknesses that need to be addressed. We have tried our best to keep essay type questions to a minimum but unfortunately essays are an important part of creating a business plan.

Identifying the strengths and weaknesses of your agency can be mentally and emotionally overwhelming. After the assessment, agencies are faced with the question that screws up most agency leaders . . . Where do I start?

My experience with 100's of agents has taught me that often, paralysis by analysis causes them to spend most of their time researching solution options instead of implementing solutions. To help with this situation, we have you classify your NO answers into three groups: *easy to implement tasks, medium difficult to implement tasks, and finally, difficult to implement tasks.* Your agency goal is to implement a solution for each NO answer. Begin with the easy to implement tasks for sections you decide are the most important for the agency.

Work through the sections in any order you like, except the *Executive Summary*, which should be done last. Any questions that do not apply to your agency should be marked with N/A or left blank. Some of the questions are labeled as *Optional* , this means that while it may not be considered an industry standard or necessity, it is something that should be considered in the future for your agency. Optional questions are generally focused on new technology that is available, but not often used by insurance agencies.

When you are finished with each section go back and look at all of your NO answers. As stated earlier, the No answers spotlight areas of weakness or concerns in your business that should be addressed in your overall business plan.

At the end of each section write a *short* essay explaining the overall strengths and weaknesses you identified within the section. Now you are ready to identify and explain how you plan to address the weakness in the Agency Goals and *Strategy Section* of the plan.

If you are an active Inspire a Nation Business Mentoring Svc. Member, use the resources contained in the Video and Document Library to help you create an implementation strategy for each identified weakness.

Business Plan Sections:

1. Executive Summary
2. General Agency Description
3. Market Analysis
4. Organizational Chart
5. Agency Staffing and Personnel
6. Marketing/Advertising
7. Customer Retention
8. Internet Technology/Social Media
9. Accountability and Tracking Tools
10. Finance
11. S.W.O.T (Strengths, Weaknesses, Opportunities, Threats)
12. Agency Goals and Strategies

The Real Value of a Business Plan!

The real value of doing a business plan is not having the finished product in hand; rather, the value lies in the process of research and thinking about your business in a systematic way. The act of planning helps you to think things through thoroughly, to study and research when you are not sure of the facts, and to look at your ideas critically. It takes time, but avoids costly, perhaps disastrous, mistakes later.

This business plan template is generic enough to use for all types of property and casualty agencies, however, you should modify it to suit your particular agency model.

Before the Inspire a Nation Business Mentoring Svc., business plan model came along it typically took several weeks to complete a good plan for an insurance agency. Now, thanks to the hard work and effort of the Inspire a Nation Business Mentoring team, you can create a thorough and effective plan in days, not weeks!

And finally, be sure to keep detailed notes on your sources of information and on the assumptions underlying your financial data.

Whether you received this template as part of your Inspire a Nation Business Mentoring membership, or you bought it outside of our membership program, you are making one of the best investments you could have selected for your agency, and more importantly you are laying the foundation that the success of your agency will be built upon for years to come.

So let's get started building your plan!

Billy R. Williams, PhD., President – Inspire a Nation Business Mentoring Svc., and Williams Family Agency Investment Group

Inspire a Nation Business Mentoring Svc.
www.inspireanation.org

Business Plan Template

OWNERS/PRINCIPALS

Business name: Your Business Name

Address: Address Line 1
                   Address Line 2
                   City, ST ZIP Code

Telephone: (111) 1111-0000

Fax: (111) 1111-0000

Email: agencyname@agencydomain.com

Executive Summary

This should be the last section you complete. We suggest that you make it two pages or less. Include everything that you would cover in a five-minute interview. Explain the fundamentals of the agency: What are the products and services you provide, who are the carriers you represent, who are your customers, who are the owners, and what do you think the future holds for your agency and the insurance industry?

(See the Market Analysis section for my viewpoint on the future of the P & C agency. My viewpoint is based on market research, scientific studies, and good old fashioned day to day paying of attention to what is happening with Williams Family Agency Investment Group partner agencies, and the member agencies of Inspire a Nation Business Mentoring.)

Make it enthusiastic, professional, complete, and concise.

If you are applying for a loan, state clearly how much you want, how you are going to use the funds, and how the money will make your business more profitable, thereby ensuring repayment.

General Agency Description

Mission Statement:

All agencies should have a brief mission statement that clearly explains the guiding principles of the agency.

I am providing the mission statement of the agencies within the Williams Family Agency Investment Group as an example:

The goal from the inception of the agency has been to work together as a team. The teams' number one priority is the customer. Our commitment to the customer is to give excellent customer care while educating and providing coverage that will cause the least amount of disruption to their quality of life should a claim occur.

While the agency understands that a customer is sensitive to price, the price of a policy or coverage must never interfere with the staff member presenting the best overall program, policy, or coverage to a prospect or customer. As an agency, we would rather lose a customer on price than to not present them with the best overall insurance options available to them. Our responsibility is to present the coverage that will best protect their quality of life should a claim occur. It is a customer's responsibility to choose what they are willing to pay for. Any staff member found to not be in compliance of the "Best overall" presentation requirement may be reassigned to a different position within the agency or immediately terminated.

As an agency and team, we strive to be a leader and role model to other agencies on a local, regional and national level. Our success as an agency is measured by profitability, customer satisfaction and the value we bring to our customers, networking partners, and the community as a whole.

The remainder of this section is mainly small essay type questions.

What is your target market?

Describe your thoughts on the insurance industry:

What is the insurance industry presently as it relates to the products and services your agency provides?

What changes do you foresee in the insurance industry?

How is your company poised to take advantage of the changes you foresee?

A detailed description of the agency:

(Note - Many questions within this section can't be answered until you have gone through the complete plan, so if you are not sure of an answer, skip it and come back to it later.)

Form of ownership: Sole proprietor, partnership, corporation, or limited liability corporation (LLC)?

What is the estimated monthly draw or compensation of each owner or agency principal? Monthly $_____

Company history: Years in business, previous owners, successes, failures, lessons learned, reputation in community, sales and profit history, number of employees, and events that affected success. Discuss significant past problems and how you solved and survived them.

Most important strengths and core competencies: What factors will make the agency succeed? What are your major competitive strengths? What strengths do you personally bring to the business?

Significant challenges the agency faces now and in the near future: If you are asking for funding, go on to explain how the new capital will help you meet these challenges.

Long term: What are your plans for the future of the agency?

You must always develop strategies for continued growth, increased sales production, increased retention results, product diversification, and the eventual transfer or sale of the agency?

Have you put plans and strategies in place to address these situations? Yes_____ No_____

If you answered YES to the question above, you will need to explain the strategies throughout this business plan. If you answered NO to the question above, developing this business plan will help you develop strategies to address those concerns.

Agency Transfer and/or Succession Strategies

(Optional) Does the agency have a Key Manager life insurance policy owned by the agency on all agency principals and key leadership? (The death benefit flows to the agency) Yes_____   No_____

(Optional) Do all agency owners have a life insurance policy that will fund the transfer of the agency to a family member or chosen successor? (The death benefit flows to the successor) Yes_____   No_____

(Optional) Has the agency principal reviewed the tax implications of the transfer of ownership of the agency with the selected successor(s) and legal/financial counsel? Yes_____   No_____

Do all key leaders within the agency have disability insurance coverage? Yes_____ No_____

Products and Services

Describe in depth the main products and services the agency provides or plans on providing to consumers:

What carriers do you use to provide the products and services, or what carriers do you plan on using?

Which products and services are your current lead item(s) for agency income and agency marketing campaigns?

Do you plan to continue the products and services mentioned above as your lead item(s) for agency income? Yes_____   No_____

If you answered NO above, what products and services will become your agency's new lead item(s)?

What factors give you competitive advantages or disadvantages? For example, the level of quality, or unique proprietary features?

How will current and future product pricing impact your competiveness in the insurance marketplace?

Market Analysis

The *Market Analysis* looks at the total insurance landscape as it relates to the agency. The Insurance Landscape is changing and agencies must be prepared to adapt to the change or face the same market upheaval that decimated many travel agencies, car dealerships and flower shops.

The major change to the landscape is coming in the form of internet based technology. While this new technology makes it easier for consumers to purchase insurance and receive service through a variety of channels, it also has an undesired effect of devaluing the importance of an insurance agent.

Major carriers are spending millions of dollars on new delivery channels that are Internet-based and often overlook or completely cut out the insurance agent. In order for insurance agencies to stay relevant in commoditized markets such as auto insurance they will have to do several things:

The following are paraphrased bullet points taken from a report by McKinsey & Company concerning the insurance industry and the future of the Property and Casualty agency model. Here is a hyperlink to the actual report. I *STRONGLY* suggest you take a moment and read the entire report before completing the Market Analysis section! The McKinsey & Company report (McKinsey & Company *is the trusted advisor and counselor to many of the world's most influential businesses and institutions)*

- Agents must move beyond the local market paradigm in which the customer base is strictly geographically defined. (for example five-mile radius centered on their office)
- Agents and agencies must become more specialized in their insurance models. With customers having free access to so much information they are not willing to pay for generalist advice for non complex transactions such as purchasing auto insurance.
- 85% of all consumers that shop for insurance start their search online by either researching information about the product and product providers, or requesting a quote or information. Agents must have an internet presence to deliver information to prospects and customers in order to stay relevant in the marketplace.
- Social media and sites such as Yelp, and Angie's list make it easy for customers to recommend and disparage businesses. Agencies must utilize these sites to grow their name and brand recognition, as well as respond to complaints and negative comments.
- The less complex the insurance need of the consumer the more likely they are to turn to Internet-based technology for the quoting and purchasing of insurance products. Auto insurance is leading the way in this new trend.

- The more complicated the policy or need to the consumer the more valuable the advice of the insurance professional becomes.
- Many insurance carriers are starting to question the value of an insurance agent in the insurance sales process because of the cost, ease, efficiency and consistent customer interaction Internet-based technology can deliver to consumers.

Agents and agencies will have to adapt to this changing landscape by:
1. implementing and embracing new technology such as electronic documents, text messaging, video conferencing, instant chat through the agency website, mobile phone marketing, review sites, and of course social media
2. actively pursuing niche markets, affinity groups, business referral partners, and expanding their geographic and demographic markets
3. Using various ways and technologies to request referrals, positive reviews, and testimonials
4. minimizing agency devaluation by growing bigger through increased customer retention, organic marketing processes, and through acquisitions, which will require agency staff to be consistent in their use of technology, processes, conversations, and servicing of customers
5. by outsourcing certain agency functions to carriers or third-party providers,
6. banding together with other small agencies and maximizing the power of economy of scale when purchasing products and services to support the agency,
7. targeting new revenue sources such as life insurance, financial services, group benefits, health insurance, and even notary services

Here are some questions that will help you complete this section:

1. Does the agency embrace new technology? Yes_____ No_____
2. If you answered NO to the question above, is it the agency's intent to try to add new technology? Yes_____ No_____
3. Does the agency market its products and services to the entire state in which it is domiciled? Yes_____ No_____
4. If you answered YES to the question above, does the agency market its products and services to multiple states? Yes_____ No_____

5. Does the agency have a specific niche or affinity group that it strongly promotes in its marketing efforts? Yes_____ No_____

6. If the agency's primary products are auto and home insurance, does the agency do a good job of cross selling life insurance? Yes_____ No_____ Financial Services? Yes_____ No_____

7. Does the agency institute a staff training/retraining program that causes a consistent customer interaction among all staff members? Yes_____ No_____

8. Which of the following technologies does the agency utilize as a part of the customer service process? Facebook? Yes_____ No_____
Agency Provided Text Messaging Technology? Yes_____ No_____
Instant Chat through the agency website? Yes_____ No_____
Click to Call Button on the agency's website? Yes_____ No_____

Agency Distribution Channels

How do you sell your products or services?

- (Optional) Retail? (outbound prospecting, walk-ins, call-ins, referrals) Yes_____ No_____

- (Optional) Direct? (Internet, complete web processing) Yes_____ No_____

- (Optional) Wholesale? Yes_____ No_____

- (Optional) Employee Agents? Yes_____ No_____

- (Optional) Independent reps? Yes_____ No_____

- (Optional) National Accounts? Yes_____ No_____

Have your distribution channels proven effective? Yes_____ No_____

Do you need to make any changes or additions to current strategies? Yes_____ No_____ If yes, what changes do you anticipate making?

FYI. . . Complete this section with your eyes focused on the future!

Organizational Chart

Management and Organization

For positions that are not working effectively, would you consider outsourcing the work generally performed by those positions? Yes_____   No_____

If you answered NO to the question above, do you plan on hiring an individual or team to handle the functions? Yes_____   No_____

If you answered no to the question above, and you are filling the majority of the roles above, do you feel you can effectively continue to operate and grow your agency without having someone else fill the roles Yes_____   No_____

Will you manage the business on a day-to-day basis? Yes_____   No_____

If you answered NO to the question above:

What is the name of the person that will manage the business on a day-to-day basis?

What experience does that person bring to the business?

What special or distinctive competencies do they possess that you feel will make them successful in the position?

Who will take over their role in the business if this person is lost or incapacitated?

Note: Modify the organizational chart above showing the management hierarchy and who is responsible for key functions. Include position descriptions for key employees.

Professional and Advisory Support

List the following:

- Board of directors and management advisory board

- Attorney

- Accountant

- Insurance agent (If you use an outside agent for asset protection)

- Banker

- Consultants

- Mentors and key advisors (Including Inspire a Nation)

Agency Production Analysis – (Based on agency reports)

If the agency has efficient production tracking tools in use, completing this section of the business plan template should be a snap. However, if there are no production tracking tools in use, this section can be nearly impossible to complete.

If you are creating this business plan to use for the purposes of getting a loan and you can't adequately complete this section, your ability to prove to a lender that your agency is viable and more importantly, has the ability to repay the loan, is greatly diminished.

We recommend that your look-back period is 12 months from the date you declare on the front page of this business plan. If you do not have a full 12 months of data, use whatever full look-back period you can verify.

Quote to Sales Volume Closing Percentages: (Total Quotes/Sales)

Total Auto Quotes:_____ Total Sales:_____ Auto Q/S %:_____

Total Property Quotes:_____ Total Sales;_____ Property Q/S %:_____

Commercial 1 Quotes:_____ Commercial 1 Sales_____ Commercial 1 Q/S %:_____

Commercial 2 Quotes:_____ Commercial 2 Sales_____ Commercial 2 Q/S %:_____

Commercial 3 Quotes:_____ Commercial 3 Sales_____ Commercial 3 Q/S %:_____

Life Insurance Quotes:_____ Life Insurance Sales:_____ Life Insurance Q/S %:____

Product 1 Quotes:_____ Product 1 Sales_____ Product 1 Q/S %:_____

Product 2 Quotes:_____ Product 2 Sales_____ Product 2 Q/S %:_____

Product 3 Quotes:_____ Product 3 Sales_____ Product 3 Q/S %:_____

Mono-line Auto BOB %:_____

Mono-line Property BOB %:_____

Top Sources of Quotes

What are the top 2 sources of new business quotes for each primary line of insurance?

Auto Quotes: Source 1_____   Source 2_____

Homeowner Quotes: Source 1_____   Source 2_____

Life Insurance Quotes: Source 1_____   Source 2_____

Commercial 1 Quotes: Source 1_____   Source 2_____

Commercial 2 Quotes: Source 1_____   Source 2_____

Commercial 3 Quotes: Source 1_____   Source 2_____

Additional Product 1 Quotes: Source 1_____   Source 2_____

Additional Product 2 Quotes: Source 1_____   Source 2_____

Additional Product 3 Quotes: Source 1_____   Source 2_____

Top Sources of Issued New Business

(Don't assume the top quoting sources are also the top issued new business sources. Use your agency reports to confirm your responses)

Auto: Source 1_____   Source 2_____

Homeowner: Source 1_____   Source 2_____

Life Insurance: Source 1_____   Source 2_____

Commercial 1: Source 1_____   Source 2_____

Commercial 2: Source 1_____   Source 2_____

Commercial 3: Source 1_____   Source 2_____

Additional Product 1: Source 1_____   Source 2_____

Additional Product 2: Source 1_____   Source 2_____

Additional Product 3: Source 1_____   Source 2_____

Agency Referral Sources

Top 3 Inside of Agency Referral Campaigns/Processes/Individuals

Source 1_____   Source 2_____   Source 3_____

Top 3 Outside of Agency Referral Sources/Partners

Source 1_____   Source 2_____   Source 3_____

Agency Retention

Overall 1ST Year Retention(All Lines):_____ (First year retention is a reflection of the agency's marketing focus, sales conversation, (expertise vs price) and the effectiveness of the New Customer Process. (The new customer process has a large impact on retention)

Overall Agency Retention:_____

Agency Premium Production

For the following report items use items or policies depending on your carrier's preferred reporting method.

Total Policies:_____   Total Premium: $_____ Commission_____

Total Auto policies Written:_____   Total Premium: $_____ Commission_____

Total Renters Policies Written:_____   Total Premium: $_____ Commission_____

Total Condo Policies Written:_____   Total Premium: $_____ Commission_____

Total Home Owners Policies Written:_____   Total Premium: $_____ Commission_____

Total Commercial Policies Written:_____   Total Premium: $_____ Commiss on_____

Total (Current) Financial Services Production Credit? $_____

Total Agency Commission (All lines of insurance)$_____

Marketing Expense:
Total amount of Money spent on marketing for the reporting period? $_____

Agency Staffing and Personnel

This section will contain a lot of questions and sub-sections, but each question will reveal strengths and weaknesses in your staffing process.

Inspire a Nation Business Mentoring stresses the importance of proper staffing and staff training. Your agency will never reach its true potential without staff being "all-in" with the agency's mission statement and actively following the designated processes.

We recommend the following:

1. You should have at a minimum one fully P&C licensed staff for every 750 households. *(Fully licensed includes life insurance and fixed financial services products)*

2. You should perform an assessment test on every candidate prior to hiring them to insure they are a good fit for the position you are hiring them to fill.

3. You should test all <u>current employees</u> when starting the Inspire a Nation Business Mentoring program. This will help engage your current staff, as well as give you some insight into their strengths and weaknesses

In general are staff duties: Specialized_____ Blended Duties_____

How would you rate staff adherence to current processes and agency operations:

Strong_____ Medium_____ Weak_____

Proper staffing is a key component to an agency's success. Proper staffing includes:
- Hiring the appropriate amount of employees for the agency's operations
- Placing the right people in the right positions based on their skill sets and personalities
- Using automation and technology to perform important tasks that would normally be performed by a staff member
- Conducting a thorough candidate interview
- Candidate Assessment Testing
- Providing an explaining the agency's Employee Handbook
- Offering a competitive salary along with bonus opportunities
- Having new hires read, sign and date a Non Compete/Non Disclosure Form
- Having staff accurately complete all tasks within the agency's On-boarding and Staff Reinforcement Training Guide
- Providing new staff with the appropriate Health Insurance Options documentation

Sub-section 1: Locating Staff

When looking for staff does your agency

1. Use staffing agencies? Yes_____   No_____

2. Identify local agencies that are for sale and/or closing and contact the principal agent to see if they will give you permission to interview staff? Yes_____   No_____

3. Use recently licensed information provided by the State Insurance Department? Yes_____   No_____   N/A_____ (The state does not provide the information)

4. Have a relationship with state approved pre-licensing and continuing education providers? Yes_____   No_____   N/A_____

5. Use staffing sites such as monster.com, or jobs.com? Yes_____   No_____

6. Post an ad in local newspapers? (including free periodicals) Yes_____ No_____

7. (Optional) Have wording on the back of your business cards that state that 'your agency is always looking to interview quality licensed and unlicensed staff?" Yes_____   No_____

8. Does your agency have an Agency Hotline with prompts explaining the positions available in the agency? Yes_____   No_____

Sub-Section 2: Interviewing Candidates

When interviewing candidates does your agency

1. Fully overview the position, including what success looks like in the position?
   Yes_____   No_____

2. Fully explain what the agency does to support success in the position including training opportunities, tracking tools and technology provided? Yes____   No____

3. Ask the candidate to provide proof of successes in similar positions such as certificates and awards? Yes_____   No_____

4. Ask the candidates about failures in similar positions and what the candidate did to rectify and eliminate future failures? Yes_____   No_____

5. Role play a typical scenario that occurs in the position to see how the candidate would handle the scenario? Yes_____   No_____

6. Instruct the candidate to take a one minute typing test? Yes_____   No_____

7. Have the candidate take a spreadsheet *usage* test? Yes_____   No_____

8. Have the candidate make a live call to a customer or prospect and follow a script the agency would typically use on that call? Yes_____   No_____

9. Have all candidates that are considered serious contenders for the position after the initial interview take an assessment test that is based on the skills needed to be successful in the position? Yes_____   No_____

Sub-Section 3: Hiring and On-boarding staff

1. Does the agency have an up-to-date employee handbook that is issued and fully reviewed with a new staff member? Yes_____   No_____

2. Does the agency use an on-boarding guide and process training program with new staff? Yes_____   No_____

3. Does the agency designate who will train, track, and sign-off on the on-boarding guide for new staff members? Yes_____   No_____

4. Has new staff been given access to, and shown how to use the Inspire a Nation Video and Document Library?

5. Does the agency have all new staff sign a non-compete and non-disclosure form? Yes_____   No_____

6. Does the agency provide the Obama Care health insurance notifications required by law to new staff? Yes_____   No_____

7. Does the agency counsel new staff members monthly on their strengths and weaknesses? (Up to the end of their probationary period) Yes_____   No_____

8. Does the agency fully explain to new staff members the general compliance situations the agency must adhere to in order to conduct business? Yes_____ No_____

9. Does the agency offer training aids and resources new staff members can utilize outside of normal work hours? Yes_____   No_____

Sub-Section 4: Staff Compensation

1. Is the general staff compensation plan clearly explained in the employee handbook? Yes_____ No_____

2. (Optional) Is the staff base compensation linked with insurance education completion? Yes_____ No_____

3. (Optional) Does the agency provide bonus options to licensed sales producers Yes_____ No_____

4. (Optional) Does the agency provide bonus options to CSRs? Yes_____ No_____

5. (Optional) Are the bonus plans for the staff members a reflection of what the agency must accomplish to earn bonus money from the carriers the agency represents? Yes_____ No_____

6. (Optional) On average do most of the agency's staff members earn a bonus during the designated bonus period? (weekly, monthly, quarterly, etc.) Yes_____ No_____

Marketing/Advertising

Every agent/agency understands the importance of effective, cost efficient, and consistent marketing and advertising campaigns. Carriers understand it a so, which is why large carriers spend millions of dollars each year on marketing and advertising.

Along with their own marketing/advertising campaigns, agencies should leverage the marketing/advertising campaigns that the carriers they represent have in place. This can often be accomplished at a much lower cost by utilizing marketing resources and materials that are provided to the agency.

In addition, most carriers offer co-op funds, monetary incentives for sales, and marketing reimbursement if specific production requirements are met by the agency.

This section of the business plan will have you answer questions that can uncover weaknesses not only in the agency's marketing efforts, but weaknesses in how effectively you work with your carrier's marketing campaigns

On a scale of 1 to 5 (1 = Excellent, 5 = Poor) How overall effective is your agency at marketing for new customers? Score_____

On a scale of 1 to 5 (1 = Excellent, 5 = Poor) How overall effective is your agency at seeking out new business opportunities during service calls? Score_____

On a scale of 1 to 5 (1 = Excellent, 5 = Poor) How overall effective is your agency at seeking out new business opportunities during policy review conversations? Score_____

Carrier Support

(Optional) What 3 insurance carriers are the most important by revenue to your agency?

Carrier 1:_____ Carrier 2:_____ Carrier 3:_____

Which of the carriers you listed above does your agency spend the most marketing money to promote to your prospects and customers?_____

Which of the carriers listed above provide the most marketing funds (upfront or on a reimbursement basis to) your agency_____

Does the carrier that the agency promotes the most provide the most marketing funds to the agency? Yes_____ No_____

If the answer to the question above is NO, Do you plan on keeping the dynamics of your marketing the same as it relates to the carrier? Yes_____   No_____

On a scale of 1 to 5 (1 = Excellent, 5 = Poor) How effectively does the agency take advantage of marketing materials provided by its carriers? Score_____

On a scale of 1 to 5 (1 = Excellent, 5 = Poor) How effectively does the agency take advantage of marketing funds provided by its carriers? Score_____

What would you list as the primary marketing/advertising platform you use to market to your customers? (I.E. mailings, telemarketing, emails, pay-per-click, etc.)

What marketing and advertising campaigns do you use, why, and how often? (I.E. new homeowners, boat owners, senior market, internet leads, etc.)

Has your current marketing/advertising been effective? Yes_____   No_____

How can you tell?
_____
_____

Marketing and Advertising Methods Used

Identify the marketing/advertising methods you use, as well as how often you use them. For *Yes* answers use a score of (1 = very often) to (5 = rarely)

- Word of mouth: Yes_____   No_____   Score_____

- Network of other professionals: Yes_____   No_____   Score_____

- Niche and/or Specialized Markets? Yes_____   No_____   Score_____

- Agency referral campaigns Yes_____   No_____   Score_____?

- Various inside of agency telemarketing campaigns? Yes_____   No_____
  Score_____

- Various outsourced telemarketing campaigns? Yes_____   No_____
  Score_____

- Drip email campaigns? Yes_____   No_____   Score_____

- Postal mail campaigns? Yes_____   No_____   Score_____

- Search engine marketing campaigns? Yes_____   No_____   Score_____

- Online Yellow Pages and similar directories? Yes_____ No_____ Score_____

- Website traffic and quotes? Yes_____ No_____ Score_____

- Google Maps and Places? Yes_____ No_____ Score_____

- Internet Leads? (Real Time and Aged) Yes_____ No_____ Score_____

- "Win Back" campaigns for former customers? Yes_____ No_____ Score_____

- Emergency Contact Processes? Yes_____ No_____ Score_____

- Birthday/Wedding Anniversary touches? Yes_____ No_____ Score_____

- Written Testimonials and Recommendations? Yes_____ No_____ Score_____

- Blogs, Press Releases, and other written material? Yes_____ No_____ Score_____

- Group Presentations? (live speaking engagements, conference calls, webinars, etc.) Yes_____ No_____ Score_____

- Billboard Marketing? (billboards, movie theaters, bus stops, yard signs, etc.) Yes_____ No_____ Score_____

- Social Media Video Marketing? (YouTube, YP.com, facebook, LinkedIn, etc.) Yes_____ No_____ Score_____

- Social Media Contacts? (testimonials, referral request, policy review reminders, etc.) Yes_____ No_____ Score_____

- Request customers post reviews on review Sites such as Google +, Yelp, and Angie's List? Yes_____ No_____ Score_____

- Trade Show Booths? Yes_____ No_____

- Non Profit/Charity Support Campaigns? (Donations to the organization's your agency supports, Pay-per-Quote, Etc.) Yes_____ No_____

- Door Knocking and Office Visits? Yes_____ No_____ Score_____

Marketing Support

Does the agency have a dedicated Marketing Assistant? Yes_____   No_____

Does the agency assign specific marketing campaigns to designated staff within the agency? Yes_____   No_____

If you answered YES to the question above, on a scale of 1 to 5 (1 = Very effective – 5 = Not effective) rate how effective the marketing/advertising campaigns are in the agency? _____

Write a short essay that explains why you gave the rating above:

_____

_____

If you answered NO to the *"assign specific marketing campaign"* question above, does the agency outsource the majority of its marketing campaigns? Yes_____   No_____

If you answered NO to the question above, does the agency primarily depend on its carriers to generate marketing for the agency? Yes_____   No_____

Marketing/Advertising Budget

How much do you plan to spend on marketing/advertising?

Monthly $_____   Quarterly $_____   Annually $_____

Should you consider spending less on some marketing activities and more on others? Yes_____   No_____

Marketing Compliance

Is the agency aware of and fully trained on the FTC and FCC Telemarketing Rules? Yes_____   No_____

Does the agency have a "Permission to Contact" process in place for customers and prospects? Yes_____   No_____

Does the agency have government issued SAN # for telemarketing calls? (Agency or carrier provided) Yes_____   No_____

Does the agency utilize a CAN-SPAM checklist when creating in-house email marketing campaigns? Yes_____   No_____

(Optional) Does the agency utilize marketing lists providers that scrub for DNC and mobile phone numbers? Yes_____   No_____

(Optional) If you answered NO to the question above, does the agency utilize a scrubbing tool (agency or carrier provided) to scrub prospecting lists for DNC and mobile phone numbers? Yes_____   No_____

Pricing

As insurance agents we rarely have a large impact on pricing. We help our prospects and customers to identify discounts they qualify to receive and independent agents can add policy and service fees in some states, but generally it is the carrier that decides the price of a policy. The inability of the agent to impact pricing one of the items that's causing a devaluation of agents and agencies in the customer's mind. In order to overcome this, agents must have strong quality and value conversations during the sales and service process.

Carriers understand that having the lowest prices is not a good strategy. Usually an insurance company will do better to have average prices and compete on ease of doing business, quality of products, and claims service.

Does your agency focus on quality and service when competing against other agencies and carriers? Yes_____   No_____

Does your agency role play various sales scenarios with the focus on redirecting a prospect's attention to the value the agency brings to the transaction? Yes_____ No_____

Compare your prices with those of your competition. Are they higher, lower, the same? Why?

On a scale of 1 to 5 (1 = Extremely Important, 5 = Not Important) How important is price as a competitive factor to the agency? Score_____

Many agencies will focus their marketing efforts on the most price sensitive of customers even when the products they offer don't align with that customer.

Does your agency's marketing efforts focus on the niches, demographics, and geographical areas that can best handle your carrier's value proposition and pricing? Yes_____   No_____

Payment Options

Research has shown that ease of doing business is of major importance to the average consumer. Primary among doing business is the type of payment options available to the consumer. It is important that agencies utilize technology available from the carriers to make it as easy as possible for a customer to apply down payments, have a variety of payment options, and have the ability to make payments online, over the phone and through mobile applications available on their phone.

In addition, consumers want to have the ability to make payments at times that is convenient for them. 24 X 7 payment options are no longer a luxury, but an industry standard. Captive agents don't generally have an issue with payment options, but there are many independent agencies that are not utilizing the payment options available to them through their carriers?

Does the agency have a variety of payment plans and options available to the consumer? Yes_____   No_____

If you replied yes to the question above, does the agency staff do a good job of thoroughly explaining the payment options during sales and service contacts with the consumer? Yes_____   No_____

(Optional) Does your agency collect policy or service fees? Yes_____
No_____

Location

Let's take a look at your location as its potential impact on your marketing.

Is your location a storefront or easily seen by the average consumer? Yes_____
No_____

If you answered NO to the question above, is your agency's focus on prospecting and servicing customers built around technology tools? Yes_____   No_____

If you answered YES to the question above, what are the technology tools you are currently using, and what tools do you plan on adding in the future?

If customers come to your place of business:

Is the parking adequate? Yes_____   No_____

Is your location consistent with the image your agency wants to portray? Yes_____
No_____

Is the rent/mortgage you are paying on your location taking away from the overall quality of the agency? (I.E. hiring new staff, marketing, upgrading technology, etc.)
Yes_____   No_____

If you answered YES to the question above, is there a plan in place to look for a different location or to try and renegotiate the current rent/mortgage? Yes_____
No_____

If you answered NO to the question above is your plan to deal with the rent/mortgage situation by getting a bank loan, write more business, cut expenses?

Where is the agency's primary competition located?

Customer Retention Section

Let's be honest, retention is the reason agency owners take the leap to start or purchase an agency.
With the changing insurance landscape, maintaining current customers is paramount to the success of the agency. Every aspect of agency operations impacts retention, so an agency must insure the entire customer experience promotes retention and has value to the customer.
Another important key to strong retention is value based communication with customers. Value based communication is communication that expresses and protects the customers best interest.
This is another section that doesn't require a long synopsis, so let's get going on the assessment questions

Communication Methods

Which of the following communication methods does the agency use to communicate with customers?

Manual Calls_____   Email_____   Drip Email_____

Automated Calls (Permission based)_____

Predictive Dialer Calls_____   Postal Mail_____   Text Message_____

Social Media Post_____   Social Media Message_____   Instant Chat_____

Website Click to Chat_____   Video Conference_____

- Does the agency have a formalized Customer Policy Cancellation/Termination Contact Process? Yes_____   No_____

If you answered YES to the question above, rate how effective the agency is at performing the Cancellation/Termination Contact Process? (1 = effective – 5 = Not effective)_____

- Does the agency have a formalized Endorsement Process? Yes_____ No_____

If you answered YES to the question above, rate how effective the agency is at performing the complete Endorsement Process? (1 = effective – 5 = Not effective)_____

- Does the agency utilize a formalized Customer Policy Review Contact Process? Yes_____ NO_____

If you answered YES to the question above, rate how effective the agency is at performing the complete Customer Policy Review Process? (1 = effective – 5 = Not effective)_____

- How many days out from a customer's renewal does the agency start the Customer Policy Review Contact Process?_____

- Does the agency request a new customer complete a "Permission to Contact" form? Yes_____ No_____

If you answered YES to the question above, rate how effectively the agency staff communicates the importance of the Permission to Contact form?
(1 = effectively – 5 = Not effectively)_____

- Does the agency have a formalized Emergency Contact Process? Yes_____ No_____

If you answered YES to the question above, rate how effective the agency is at performing the complete Emergency Contact Process? (1 = effective – 5 = Not effective)_____

- Are new customers briefed about Customer Policy Review notices and when to expect reminders? Yes_____ No_____

- Are new customers contacted within 7 business days of becoming a new customer to verify the policy issued and to up-sell/cross-sell based on the agency's concern about weaknesses in their insurance profile? Yes_____ No_____

- Does the agency utilize a formalized Claims Process? Yes_____ No_____

If you answered YES to the question above, rate how effective the agency is at performing the complete Claims Contact Process? (1 = effective – 5 = Not effective)_____

- Does the agency have a predetermined rate increase % that triggers a rate increase contact from the agency? Yes_____ No_____

If you answered YES to the question above, rate how effective the agency staff has been about completing the *Rate Increase Contact Process*? (1 = effective – 5 = Not effective)_____

- Does the agency have a formalized *Birthday Contact Process* for customers? Yes_____ No_____

If you answered YES to the question above, rate how effective the agency is at performing the *Birthday Contact Process*? (1 = effective – 5 = Not effective)_____

- (Optional) Does the agency outsource any of the retention processes mentioned above? Yes_____ No_____

If you answered yes to the question above, which processes are currently outsourced?

(Optional) Do you feel the agency should outsource any additional retention processes? If yes, which processes?

- Does the agency regularly have training and role play dedicated to the retention processes mentioned above? Yes_____ No_____

Internet Technology and Social Media

Internet Technology (I.T.) is an often overlooked but very important part of an agency's operations.

For the purposes of this business plan, I.T. encompasses much more than just making sure your computers are working properly. This section will ask questions about internet based technologies that you might not normally consider an I.T. topic, but because new technology, internet based tools, and web based programs are becoming such an important part of an agency's operations, there is a need to put them in this section to make sure they have been discussed. Many of the questions below might have been answered in a previous section of the business plan, but answer them here as well for easy identification of I.T. weaknesses and concerns.

Current Computer Systems and Capacity

1. What is the total number of computers operating in a business capacity within the agency?_____

2. Do the computers in your agency have up-to-date software such as Internet Explorer, Adobe flash, and soundcards? Yes_____   No_____

3. Does the agency have an external data back-up plan in place?

4. If you wanted to bring on additional staff do you have enough computers to support that? Yes_____   No_____

5. Who is your internet provider?

6. What are the current Push_____ and Pull_____ speeds your internet provider gives you? _____

7. Do feel your current internet provider is adequate for your current and future business operations? Yes_____   No_____

8. If you answered NO to the question above have you started to look at other Internet providers? Yes_____   No_____

9. Do you have a WebCam and microphone on the computers in your agency? Yes_____   No_____

10. Do you currently have VOIP in your agency? (Voice over Internet Protocol)

    Yes_____   No_____

11. Do you have a maintenance contract for the computers and Internet service in your agency? Yes_____   No_____

12. Do you have an IT budget in your agency? Yes_____   No_____

Current Technology in Use:

1. (Optional for Captive Agencies) Do you use an online rater in your agency?

   Yes_____   No_____

2. Does your agency utilize an agency management system? Yes_____

   No_____

3. If you answered YES to the two questions above, does your rater information automatically download into your agency management system? Yes_____

   No_____

4. If you answered NO to the question above, is your staff efficient at manually transferring information from your rater to your agency management system?

   Yes_____   No_____

5. Do you have an active data backup system in place? Yes_____   No_____

6. (Optional) Does the agency utilize fillable Accord Forms with customers, prospects, and carriers? Yes_____   No_____

7. Does the agency utilize email to communicate with prospects, customers, and carriers? Yes_____   No_____

8. Does the agency have a domain name? (i.e. @bestinsurance.com) Yes_____

   No_____

9. Have you registered your domain name with multiple social media and websites on the internet? (i.e. www.knowem.com) Yes_____   No_____

10. Do all e-mails sent from the agency utilize the agency's domain name as opposed to a non-business domain such as Gmail or Yahoo? Yes_____

    No_____

11. Does the agency use *Drip Email* to communicate important topics and prospecting information to customers and prospects? Yes_____   No_____

12. Does the agency have a website?

13. Does the website allow a prospect to input quote information on the website? (A quote form) Yes_____   No_____

14. (Optional) Can a prospect complete the entire insurance purchase process on your website? (Quote – Complete the application – E-sign forms – Pay - Receive a binder) Yes_____   No_____

15. Does the agency have a YouTube video(s) that tells about the agency? Yes_____   No_____

16. Does the website have a testimonials page? Yes_____   No_____

Social Media

- Does the agency have a business facebook page? Yes_____   No_____

- Does the agency have a company LinkedIn page? Yes_____   No_____

- (Optional) Does the agency have a Blog? Yes_____   No_____

- Does the agency ask customers to write recommendations and testimonials on any social media or online review site such as google+, Yelp, etc.? Yes_____   No_____

- How does the agency let customers know about its social media pages? (Check all that apply)

  Staff Conversations_____   Brochures/Flyers_____   Individual Email_____

  Drip Email_____   Website Link_____   Blog Link_____   QR Code_____

  Marketing Materials_____

Additional Technology

- (Optional) Does the agency utilize an agency based text messaging program to communicate with customers and prospects? Yes_____   No_____

- Does the agency utilize Electronic Signature software? Yes_____   No_____

- Does the agency utilize *QR Codes* to allow customers to scan agency information using their smart phones? (i.e. facebook like request, agency contact information, mobile phone permission to contact verification, etc.) Yes_____   No_____

Does the agency offer any type of *mobile app* to customers? Yes_____   No_____

Here are two mobile apps that the agency can introduce to its customer base.
WreckCheck Mobile App – iPhone   Android
MyHomeScr.app.book Mobile App – iPhone   Android

Search Engine Optimization

Is there a person or a company that is responsible for the agency's Search Engine Optimization? Yes_____   No_____

(Optional) Does the agency utilize any Pay-per-Click Marketing? Yes_____   No_____

What do you feel is the major challenge the agency faces when it comes to Internet technology?

What do you feel is the major challenge the agency faces when it comes to Social Media?

Accountability and Tracking Tools

Tracking the performance and results of a process or task is the only way to validate its effectiveness and value to an agency. **DON'T** implement a process unless the agency is committed to using the tracking forms or tools associated with the process or task!

The purpose of accountability and tracking is to:
- Increase the likelihood of a reproducible outcome
- Identify areas of weakness and training opportunities
- Keep all functions and sections of the agency in sync and efficient
- Keep staff focused on the important tasks and steps within a task that add value to the customer and the agency
- Easily identify the return on investment of a staff member, tasks, process, or campaign
- Keep the agency compliant with all rules, regulations, and requirements

It is the belief of Inspire a Nation Business mentoring that the agency should automate as many of the accountability and tracking processes as possible. This will make the entire process easier, more efficient, and most importantly, the accountability and tracking stands a much greater chance of actually happening in the agency.
If agency leadership will not supervise and review manual accountability and tracking tools, automated tracking tools must be utilized in order to maximize the agency's potential.

- Does the agency regularly use accountability and tracking tools? Yes_____ No_____

- Does the agency primarily utilize manual accountability and tracking tools (spreadsheets, paper documents) or automated accountability and tracking tools (agency management systems, automated lead management systems)_____

- Mark the processes below that have a tracking and accountability log or tool that is utilized and reviewed by agency leadership:

Marketing Results_____   Lead/Quote Management_____   New Sales_____

Customer Notes/History_____   Prospect X-Date/Follow-up Dates_____

Retention Results_____   Billing Reports_____   Payments_____

Endorsements_____   Trailing Documents_____   Remittance_____

Process Steps_____   Training Schedule_____ Staff Performance_____

Agency Accounting_____   Agency Payroll_____

Does the agency utilize an on-boarding manual when bringing on new staff? Yes_____   No_____

Does the agency have a process manual that explains each of the major processes the agency staff performs in an average day? Yes_____   No_____

In each 12 month period does the agency have a designated retraining period (usually two weeks) where each process in the agency is reviewed and retrained? Yes_____   No_____

Finance

In this section I will introduce you to various financial statements you can and should use in the agency. I am providing a hyperlink that will take you to a downloadable version of the statements.

Personal Financial Statement

Click here to download a Personal Financial Statement

https://templates.office.com/en-us/Financial-Management

Underfunding of a business is one of the main reasons a business fails. Agency owners often have to draw on personal assets to finance the agency. An accurate personal financial statement will disclose what is available. Bankers, lenders, and investors will usually ask borrowers to cosign or personally guarantee any business loans.

12 month Profit and Loss Statement

Click here to download a 12 month Profit and Loss Statement
https://templates.office.com/en-us/Financial-Management

This statement is used to estimate your agency's income and expenses.

Cash Flow Projection

Click here to download a Cash Flow Projection
https://templates.office.com/en-us/Financial-Management

This template allows the small business user to project their cash flow over a 12-month period and then compare it to actual numbers.

Break-Even Analysis

Click here to download a Break-Even Analysis
https://templates.office.com/en-us/Financial-Management

This template forecasts the break-even point and the sales volume level needed to achieve a profit goal. The break-even point is the sales volume that is sufficient to cover both fixed and variable costs. At the break-even point the company does not produce a profit or loss - it simply earns just enough revenue to cover all costs.

S.W.O.T. Analysis

Click here to download a modifiable S.W.O.T. Analysis Worksheet
https://templates.office.com/en-us/Business

You have done a lot of work, answered a lot of questions, and realized some things about your agency that you were completely unaware of. Some of the things were good, some were bad, but all of them were important.

Now it's time to review all of the answers you provided on the assessment part of this business plan and develop a S.W.O.T. Analysis. Be completely honest and objective.

Evaluate your company against your competition with using the SWOT (Strengths, Weaknesses, Opportunities, and Threats) analysis method. This worksheet template has room to compare your company against three competitors.

Agency Goals and Strategies

Now you are ready to take your agency to the next level! You have identified what's holding you back, and now it is time to identify some agency goals and to implement the exact strategies you need to put in place to accomplish those goals.

Here is the easiest way to get started shaping or reshaping your agency:

1. Select one section of the business plan you want to start working on. (Human nature will tell you that you need to start working on all of the sections at the same time, but I promise you "it will not work!" review all of your **NO** answers in that section. This will pinpoint where your agency has weaknesses.
2. Select 2 (two) weaknesses from your chosen section that you feel will be simple and easy to correct.
3. Then select 2(two) weaknesses that you feel will be a little more challenging to correct but not extremely difficult.
4. Finally select 2 (two) weaknesses that you know will be difficult to change, but the effort will be worth it to you and the agency. (Usually the most difficult item to change in an agency is staff's conversation with customers and prospects. Keep this in mind when selecting which weaknesses to address)
5. Develop a goal and a strategy for the 2 (two) simple to fix weaknesses and get them taken care of. This is important because it will give you and your staff a feeling of accomplishment and it will build some momentum and positive energy for the next more difficult tasks or processes to implement.
6. Next, develop a goal and a strategy for the medium difficulty weaknesses you want to fix. Get those knocked out as soon as possible.
7. *Here is where I need you to pay close attention to my directions. Instead of starting on the difficult tasks or weakness from the first section you chose, I want you to select another section and choose 2 (two) easy to fix weaknesses.*
8. *Start working the difficult to fix weaknesses from the first section and the easy to fix weaknesses from the second section and implement your strategy for all four.*

Let me explain why I recommend you do it this way. This will always give you and your team a sense of accomplishment and momentum, and more importantly, your progress will not stop because you are feeling beat down by the difficult weakness. Always try to work an easy (or medium if you have run out of easy to fix weaknesses)

If you are an active Inspire a Nation Business Mentoring member, this section will not be difficult for you. All you need to do is identify which weakness you want to address, search for the topic in the video library, watch the mentoring session that covers the weakness you selected, download the step-by-step job aids associated with the session, and fix the weakness. If this is a process based weakness, you can use the Data and Marketing Center CRM to implement processes with a couple of mouse clicks.

I still recommend that you always work some easy to fix weaknesses with some difficult to fix items.

I am going to use the *Retention Section* as an example for you to follow

Section: Retention -
Easy to fix weakness 1: Not calling customers that are in a late payment status
Easy to fix weakness 2: Not having a predetermined rate increase % that triggers an agency contact

Section Retention
Medium difficulty weakness 1: We don't have a formalized new customer process
Medium difficulty weakness 2: We don't notify our customers of their upcoming renewal

Section Retention
Difficult to fix weakness 1: We don't train or role play in the agency
Difficult to fix weakness 2: No one in the agency is tech savvy. I need to hire a Marketing Assistant

RETENTION GOALS

FIRST YEAR CUSTOMER RETENTION OF 85% AND HIGHER

RUN CANCELLATION/TERMINATION AUDITS WEEKLY AND CONTACT THOSE ON THE LIST

A STRONG NEW CUSTOMER ON-BOARDING PROCESS. WE WILL USE THE INSPIRE A NATION NEW CUSTOMER PROCESS

CONDUCT CPR ANNUALLY TO EDUCATE ON POLICY WEAKNESSES, RE-ESTABLISH AGENCY VALUE, AND INCREASE OR ADD PROTECTION BASED ON NEEDS

THE AGENCY WILL CREATE AN AGENCY VIDEO THAT WILL BE POSTED ON THE AGENCY WEBSITE, SOCIAL NETWORKING, AND GIVEN TO NEW CUSTOMERS AND CUSTOMER POLICY REVIEW PARTICIPANTS IN THE FORM OF A DVD OR CD.

RETENTION STRATEGIES

EASY TO FIX WEAKNESS - STRATEGY ONE

Call customers on Wednesday's that are in a late payment status

EASY TO FIX WEAKNESS - STRATEGY TWO

Contact customers that have a 5% or higher rate increase on their policy

MEDIUM DIFFICULTY WEAKNESS – STRATEGY ONE

Start implementing the Inspire a Nation Business Mentoring – New Customer Process (The tasks are simple, but getting staff to change the way they are used to doing things is what makes this a medium difficulty task.)

MEDIUM DIFFICULTY WEAKNESS – STRATEGY TWO

Set up a drip email schedule to notify customers of their upcoming policy renewal. I have to assign one of the staff and track their progress on this task. We will start with the emails we currently have in our database

DIFFICULT TO FIX – STRATEGY ONE

Retrain the staff on how to properly explain our Customer Policy Review Process, including *when* the customer should expect notifications, and how they will receive the notifications (mail, email, text, etc.)

DIFFICULT TO FIX – STRATEGY TWO

I need to hire someone that can create an agency video, post it on YouTube, and create a DVD of the agency video that we will give to new customers

The Final Step

Now take all of the information that you have just put together and go back to the top and write your Executive Summary.

We suggest that you make it two pages or less. Include everything that you would cover in a five-minute interview.

Explain the fundamentals of the agency: What are the products and services you provide, who are the carriers you represent, who are your customers, who are the owners, and what do you think the future holds for your agency and the insurance industry?

Summary

Your business plan should change as your agency changes. Review your plan once a year and make whatever adjustments need to be made. It is a GPS that when used properly will help you identify the most efficient route to your agency goals, the detours that can slow down or stop your agency's growth, and where road construction, though it is a pain in the rear, is necessary to keep your agency on course for the long haul and not just this week, month, or year.

I put hours of love and labor into creating this business plan template. It is guiding my business path in the insurance industry and I hope you allow it to do the same for you and your agency. I also hope that if you are an active Inspire a Nation Business Mentoring member that you fully utilize the resources inside of the Video and Document Library to help you implement the strategies you outlined in this plan.

If you are not an active Inspire a Nation Business Mentoring member, I hope you take a few moments to go to our website www.inspireanation.org and see what we are all about!

Billy R. Williams, PhD
President – Inspire a Nation Business Mentoring & Williams Family Agency Investment Group